THE BODY HE LEFT BEHIND

THE BODY HE LEFT BEHIND

poems

REESE CONNER

Cider Press Review
San Diego

THE BODY HE LEFT BEHIND

Cider Press Review
PO BOX 33384
San Diego, CA, USA
ciderpressreview.com

First edition
10 9 8 7 6 5 4 3 2 1 0

ISBN: 9781930781597
Library of Congress Control Number: 2021941915
Original cover illustration "Levitating Boat with Apparition of a Cat"
    by Seth Fitts
Author photograph by Mimi Tyree
Book design by Caron Andregg

Winner of the 2020 Cider Press Review Editors' Prize Book Award
ciderpressreview.com/bookaward.

Printed in the United States of America
at Bookmobile in Minneapolis, MN USA.

For dad and the cats we've loved.

Contents

The Artist

for Dante Gabriel Rossetti

He wrote poems for his wife
and, when she died young,

he buried the only copies
with her. Everyone said

it was a lovely gesture.
And isn't that why

it was a lovely gesture?
Years later, he dug up her grave

and published the contents.

Thank You

His name was Lewis
and my father loved him

            the way men
            of his generation,

            men who are not women,
            men who need to make
            that distinction

            love,

which is to say my father
met our neighbor,
received the bag
full of Lewis,

            who,
            like all dead cats
            that are carried,
            became broken rubber bands
            heavy as ball bearings,

and said *thank you*

            as if it were a kindness
            to yank a dog
            from the cat it killed,
            as if the trespass of a cat
            ought to end like this,

while that dog,
a chained-up shepherd,
still choked itself
over and over,
trying to admire
what it had done.

How to Make a Ghost

As I watch your palms
press weight on my chest—
your arms, awkward pistons
punching at my heart—
I remember the last time
on this kitchen floor
our hearts were hummingbirds.
It was years ago, before years
of baking cheese, years of cleaning,
years of avoiding mud, avoiding
tracking it on the tile, years of keeping
time, years of moving more slowly
every year, years of occasionally
sliding in socks, years now
bookended by that sex
and this moment—
a lovely discrepancy
too early for you
to appreciate. You,
who are too close
to keeping me alive, too intent
to realize it's over—
yes, too early, too soon
to remember just yet,
while your breath
is the only breath that will,
and will ever,
billow my lungs, again.
For now, it's good to see you love
the body I left behind.

To Name a Cat

I have seen a cat most days clawing at the bark of an ageless tree.
The milky husks of his lost claws stud the trunk like ghost teeth.

I have seen a cat harangue nighttime. It is his caterwaul.
He has used it on laundry, too—he doesn't discriminate.

I have seen a cat, and named him. I have known to name a cat
is to take what he is, stencil in that place an idea of cat,

then fill that with women I've loved. It is unforgivable
and precise—we have all done it.

Immediately, I have seen my cat grow old. I have traced his skeleton—
it swells like thick corduroy beneath his fur.

I have seen my cat resurrect, coming back less and less
able to bend. Old cat made of bird bone and balsa.

I have seen my cat desiccate into leather shaped like cat.
He is wrapped in black but given the burden of never seeing

the dark—it's no wonder he is afraid of it.

The Things Fathers Get to Remember

When I was young, I licked his forehead,
promising myself that he thought
I was his father. Day after day, I wet
his fur with my mouth. It was unpleasant
to taste him, but I continued,
as fathers who love their sons do,
because I needed him
to believe my mouth belonged there.

Years later, my own father told me
how he watched me lick the cat,
how he allowed me to be weird.
My father's gesture is a lovely one,
but there is blackmail in nostalgia—
the way the cat suffered my kindness,
the way torture can be a lovely gesture,
the way fathering is sometimes both.

My First Body Is Beautiful Until

after Samantha Gee's "Portrait of the Artist's Kitchen"

On the kitchen floor, years ago,
peeled potatoes roll, slippery
as skulls—all the ugliness
sticks to their wet flesh and
it's hard not to see analogy in that.

I tickle static into my first body—
it rises brightly, rises from the kitchen
and begins to tend to half-crescent stains
on counters, to supper dishes in the sink,
to routines necessary even in nostalgia.

I begin making mashed potatoes. I start
by peeling, scalping with a knife.
It's fun to see how perfectly round
I can make them. They feel so slick
to shift in my hand. My first body
is a celebration of touch because
my first body has no reflection—
it has not been urged to see one yet.

It is my birthday and I am about
to try on a new pair of checkered
pink pants. But they don't fit—
my hips are too wide now
and I trip trying to squirm in.
The thud calls my grandmother,
who comes expecting something
broken, but finds, instead,

my first body for the last time
and offers it its first reflection:
And aren't you chunky.

All this while, the ancient skulls hide
beneath the refrigerator. I left them there
because they were broken
the moment they kissed earth. Like
all disappointments, they deserved
a hiding place, so I nudged them.

Looking into Lake Erie

I do not see myself, exactly.
I see myself, inexactly.
The seaweed debris
and filthy-yellow foam
rocks in the waves
and in my way.
The surface is not clear.
Floating bits of willow bark
decorate the flashes
of sky and shore I see.
The water billows,
breaks on sheer rock
and I am sprayed—

It's cold,
too cold for August.
The clouds above
are wisps of gray
dissolving into sky.

Forgive Me, I Am a Violent Shape

The buckshot filled her wing with weight—
little steel balls nestled at the bottom
of a dozen violent hollows.
There'd be no more flying for her.

Her frame felt thick in my fist—like rubber
stretched taut over a clench of ribs, whispering
quietly with organs. Her feathers, no more
than a slippery afterthought
outside the awe of flight.

I imagined her toothpicked skeleton within,
more balsa than bone, really—
it would only take a gentle squeeze
until the *snap*.

For now, her body trembles like language.
The final instinct is always a confession,
some primordial understanding
between predator and prey.

Here is her confession:
absolute humility—the epiphany
that free will can be co-opted.
And here is mine: I am the reason

the cat, domestic and heavy
with wet food, still kills

the cockroach—tears it limb
by limb by limb by limb. He's waiting,

waiting, imposing acquiescence.
Forgive him, he is a violent shape.
I slide my thumb up the back of her neck
to the top of her skull and press firmly
until she gives.

The Things We Keep

You are beautiful and not only
in immediate ways. When
I look closer, as later on I will,
I'll be impressed with your lack
of imperfections. You wear lotion,
which makes you soft. It also makes
you slick. It is equal parts pleasant
and unpleasant to touch you.
I will keep this unpleasantness—
a privacy, a small martyrdom
we'll call a courtesy. The truth is
I do it because I care for you,
care enough to let you stay
unaware. But another truth is
I swell to know the things
I keep for you, the things
I keep from you.

Look How Obedient They Are

after Ellen Nemetz's "Lost in Translation"

Before us, needles of moonlight
clot in the fog, illuminating
this circus of animals, spellbound
and arranged like a section
of food chain: bull, coyote,
bobcat, roadrunner—impossibly
stacked in the old taxonomy.

The human is missing, though.
No one doubts he was here—
this is his architecture,
after all. He heaved it into existence
because he liked making lists, because
his belly was full of stencils
where the animals might fit
with a bit of elbow grease
and discipline. Look

how obedient they are—careful
to hold the pose, his translation
of what bodies ought to be: muscles
hushed or robust, depending; ribs, slack;
eyes, soft and glazed like warm breath
on a cold mirror. They are heavy
and domestic and content
in the template. Each animal, stiff
in a temporary heaven. But,
this is not the heaven of animals,

and they do not need to die
to become taxidermy—they are
already what he wants.

Even in this dream, his truths remain:
You must be well-fed to be wild—
a hungry thing will become
anything he wants it to.
And, these days,
all the animals are hungry.

The Rapture

after Robert Dash's "Into the Mystic"

The first thing to go was a sailboat.
It was raptured, just like that. Snap
your fingers, please. Like *that*.

An old couple watched from the end
of a pier. Beyond them, the sloop
tickled water for a bit, shuddered
like nostalgia or blackmail, then *poof*:
The mainsail, the headsail, the hull,
all the boat jargon lost specificity
like a ghost, bleeding form
and crying vowels. The boat
peeled from the water, stretching
a paintbrush of pixels in its wake
as it rose. The skyline, too,
began to glaze, and the sea
poured upward into it, everything
a swarm of movement.

Imaginative men who witnessed it
thought things like *justice*.
The old couple joined hands now.
And everyone who knew Robert Hass
knew he was right: everything
was dissolving, spiriting away
towards a more perfect self
of itself. As more world
blurred upward—housecats, tire swings,
entire orchards—a gentle murmur
spread in the bellies of the observant,

who saw even the ugly things
begin to ascend—blobfish, Smart Cars,
murder weapons, every issue of *Us Weekly*—
and thought, or began to think:
What about us? And they were all
naked now, they noticed—
clothes lifted from them
like water in a dry heat. Some ogled
the newly-naked world with intention.
Others began to tantrum—violent
or existential, all unable to translate
what must have felt like betrayal.
And that old couple, still holding hands,
looked skyward and stood up
on their tippy toes.

Self- Portrait

In the photograph, I am the body
I will always be. Even now,
when I conjure self -portrait,
I am that first body, I am the last time
I felt whole, when I hadn't yet partitioned
what I was from what I *thought*—
my bones were a name
as much as anything else.

Tonight, I return to that body, slip its skin,
nestle back into boyhood. This is celebration
long overdue. Once, I begged this body away,
embarrassed by its edges, the way
it didn't fit, the way a stranger could make it
fistfuls of flesh, the way a bend
could line too many times, could become
a surprise of gills slit into stomach, chin,
into the curl of an elbow, even.

The truth is I am lonely for my first body
and I wish I could reach back to touch it,
tell it: *I'm sorry, I'm sorry*—
you are the reflection I choose.

Significance

Someone will say we're
especially prone to gravity—
it seems to be true.
They'll say it's what makes
falling inevitable, flying
considerable. They'll say
it's what bows skeletons,
pinpoints kneecaps on femurs,
rug-burns bone to bone,
which, they'll say, is what
it means to carry weight.

The Body He Left Behind

It's time to let go
of the body he left behind,
the one that's lodged
in your eye like a floater,
a heat-waved smudge
swimming peripheries,
blurring, inhabiting, always
trying to fill
your field of view
with a tint of *him*.

I don't like the way
the body distracts, the way
you've taken it, sharpened it
into menace, and stuck it
between your shoulder blades
where it has nestled
like a knife—you've adjusted
to the betrayal.

That body's become darkness,
an ink in the water
you are drowning in.
You are inches
from the surface, clawing
in the wrong direction.

Yes, it's time to let go
of the body he left behind.
It's lodged

in your throat—
you mistake it
for breath.

My Neighbor's Cat

I didn't learn his name
until the day I buried him.
My neighbor, grief-drunk,
knocked at my door, said
the desert ground would not give,
would not help hide him
from her. *My Monkey,* she kept saying,
My Monkey. Monkey—a laughable thing
to call a cat, but it fit
the way I remembered him, too:
a black & white ricochet,
slamming invisibly against
his next impulse—almost
philosophical if you think
about it, the way he burst
this way and that, it was only
a matter of instinct
before he urged
toward the brightness
of knives, forgetting, beautifully,
the sharpness. I'm being
misleading about the knives:
It was a car. A beige one, at that.
She said it was probably
Monkey's fault, given his philosophy
of zigzags, but the driver,
that driver didn't stop, so maybe
it was sadder than she thought.
And wasn't that an odd thing
to say about sadness? Still truthful, though.

Had the driver slowed, stopped,
gotten down on her knees
to loom over the mess
she had made of Monkey,
had she cradled him, absorbed
the dull shakes of his dying,
had she kissed him softly
on the soft of his skull,
would that have been better
than driving away? And Monkey,
would he have still been afraid
of a stranger even after,
even right before?

For a Cat

Tonight, he will circle, circle, plop beside
to sleep with me one final time.
After, he'll wake to see what seethes beneath
his scabbed forepaw. It will hurt, so he will lick.
It is the logic he knows, but it will not work.
He'll lick. It will blue. He'll lick. It will bulb.
He'll lick. It will burst thick ooze, which will dry
and mat his paw with stiff, crinkly clumps
of blood in fur. The rupture will scare him,
and he'll scuttle to the closet's cubbyhole,
to the underbelly of the bed,
but last, he'll curl beneath the Oakwood desk
as if death wouldn't know where old cats hide.

For now, I see him bathe beneath the warmth
of the kitchen skylight. He sprawls while bits
of dust and fuzz float in and out of focus
above him—a sluggish mist in the sunlight.
I lay my face against his chest to hear
his gurgling insides, his thrumming purr.
I look into his tabbied face. His furred edges
ignite into a white, brilliant corona. His ears
flush with the ivy of branching veins.
His fur smells like dander and ambrosia.
He wriggles beneath me. I let him go.

The Magic

for Brian Bender

Show me your trick
    I will practice

saying it's mine
    the lie will fill my mouth

like peanut butter
    stubborn with dentures

but I'll adjust my jaw
    to learn to like

the extra teeth
    the new slur of language

the way your voice
    quietly becomes mine

until a little like you
    sounds a little like me

I'll adjust to ownership
    until each pricked finger

trickles my blood not yours
    until each tipped glass

28

spills wine as if to say
        something terrible

happened here
        I'm afraid to look

Misunderstanding

I had been good incorrectly,
and my lover told me so,
so I roared—it's all I knew to do
to interrupt the conversation
regarding tablespooning
the baking soda
which should have been
the baking powder
which should have been
measured in teaspoons, anyway,
but I only meant
to tell her

       I'd broken
father's kaleidoscope
for the first time
in my series of umpteenth times,
again, and that I was sorry
to have done it, again,
and sorry, too, to have to tantrum,
but there was a protocol—after all

I had only wanted to see myself
jigsawed into stained glass—
things felt more comfortable
that way. I never meant for it
to slip, for it to break
into rainbow shavings
in the bathroom sink,

but a clumsy moment
seemed less important
than epiphany.

When father, intent
on the expectation
of broken things, found me,
I expected to be praised.

The Chipmunk

The chipmunk, heavy
with uneven mangle
where a right shoulder
ought to be, scuttles
in spirals on the axis
of a still-attached limb.

Lewis brought her here,
to my doorstep,
the necropolis of rodents
and other gifts. Lewis will wait
with the dying chipmunk, urging
her to move differently,
willing her back
to the life he took
so that his purchase
might be made again
with another pounce,
another hunt, but
he bit too deep,
deep enough to just corrupt
the skeleton—impossibly
made of toothpicks.
The chipmunk slugs
around, around—
a broken vulture
circling itself.

After,
Lewis, head atilt, darts a paw
at the still chipmunk, no longer
a chipmunk, really. I impose
his curiosity, and why not
when he paws the dead thing
the way he does? Curiosity
is the generous imposition.

I bend down, scoop my gift.

Broken Alchemy

Miles off the coast, lightning
fistfights the sea. From this far,
most violence is also beautiful.
She smiles, naming the bright jabs
after past lovers. She doesn't
mean anything by it, but he'll remember
all the names, which is to say
he will trespass into her nostalgia
and he will alter
until each of her lovers
feels like betrayal—we've all done this.

The storm hulks toward them
like the heavy-handed metaphor. Still,
they politely refuse its superstition.
He begins to explain his trespass—
how what he knows is his fault
is her fault. Of course, she is convinced.
That is the way with lovers—they are
broken alchemy, transforming gold
into anything else. A booming vowel
brights the night, collapses a large tree
in the yard—another metaphor, perhaps.
She reaches for him and calls his name,
ending her list in a lovely reflex, but

he is too intent on avoiding endings
not to see one here. What he ought to say
is that his urge to keep a thing precious
ultimately became the fear

of losing that thing. What he ought to say
is that he's afraid Frost was right about gold,
about every type of happiness ending
in a quiet violence. What he ought to say
is that he's sorry—that it's not too late
for this to be a love poem.

Later, when the skies clear,
no one mistakes it for analogy.

The Necessary

after Andrew Hudgins' "Courtesy"

To be clear, he is not a monster.
He simply decided that progress
meant putting things
where they do not belong
until they seem to. He began: Gasoline
in automobiles, atoms in bombs, concrete
everywhere. In time, it's almost as if
his decisions are not decisions at all—
each change, the inevitable escalation
in an endless pursuit of up.

Of course, there are costs
for the misplaced things.
He knew there would be. He decides
the costs, too, are inevitable.
Still, he is most careful, so he prioritizes:
Nuclear radiation, oil pollution,
roadkill cats. All necessary
inconveniences, he decides.

Of course, he knew there was another existence,
one where the cat did not need to drag
her half-smeared self to the shoulder of a highway.
But if roads, cars, and quick commutes
mean one, two, one thousand dead cats, then
the choice is still clear: It would be far too expensive,
not to mention logistically irresponsible,
to make cat-retardant roads, so, of course,
a run-over tabby or two is a necessary

unpleasantness. He is quite sure of it.
In fact, it is silly to even say, to point out
that this cat is a choice. Yes, he resolves,
it is silly to say, even though it is true,
that this dying cat is a choice, a good choice,
that he has made,

and yet, in the next moment—the one
when she can't crawl any farther,
when he is too afraid to touch her
because she is more spillage than cat,
when he knows he'll never hear
the thrum of her purr again—he'll think
he's made the wrong choice.

Bring Flowers to What You Love

I am aggressive tonight. Bring flowers
to the cemetery. Let's dance on the graves
of men buried beneath the tombstones
bearing the funniest names. Please
do not laugh. Dance to bully the dead.
They'll feel alive, again. Leave the flowers
as a suggestion of regret. The dead
deserve small courtesies like that.

          *   *   *

One truth about grief is that no one will know
how to hug when it matters, when anything red
leads to a wound, when every wound
leads to a metaphor about scarring
or improvement or how it's only a matter of time
before the body he left behind is no longer
lodged in my eyeball like a floater,
a heat-waved smudge swimming peripheries,
blurring, inhabiting, always trying to fill,
tinting everything *him*. And isn't that
the scariest thing? He is always and never.

          *   *   *

Advice is terrible because who the hell are they?

          *   *   *

Here is my best advice about death:
Laugh at it. If you do not, you do not
understand the humor in menace.

*   *   *

I am lonely for my father.

Like a Gift

for Lewis

In this dream, I'm still hugging his body
in the front yard, hiding him
from the neighbor's dog
who sees him as a movement
to be stopped. I can feel his instinct
urge against captivity, his skeleton
bubbling to the surface—bone and claw
and fear bottled in my arms. I wonder
if I am different than the dog to him.
I wonder at what moment his instinct
to run from the dog becomes an instinct
to run from me, and I wonder, too,
how many monsters suffocate
the things they love, and how many
call it kindness. I know, I know
it's not quite so simple, but
it shouldn't be so obvious, either—
the notion that a man may keep a thing
from its own instincts on the basis
of good intentions and the power
to impose them. And I know, I know
the dog just wants to see what's inside,
and gnashing with a fistful of teeth
is the only way she knows to find out.
Still, I wonder if she comprehends
permanence, that, when she's done,
she'll never get to unwrap him,
like a gift, again.

A Little Like Desire

There is a cat somewhere
whose instinct is wind,
whose body is an orange leaf
skittering across a road—
we know what happens
to hypothetical cats
crossing roads. Yes,
there are cats that make it
to the other edge,
but all cats stalk towards
an alternative—a *snap*—
even if the car is not a car,
but cancer, bulbous,
and too menacing to belong
on the forepaw, even if the snap
is not an instant of splinter sounds,
but a gentle squeeze—a hug,
at first—escalating,
as even gentle things do.
At least the car, perhaps
the cancer, even, had intent,
which is a little like desire—
and desire, even with menace,
has meaning,
which a dying thing deserves.

Dead Tiger

You are a puddle of pretty fur,
pooling so that every bit of you
touches the ground because that
is what the dead things do—spill.

But now is no time to get maudlin.
Already, your eyes suggest nothing
I want—they are soft globes,
glazed like hot breath
on a cold mirror. A tiger
does not deserve soft eyes,
even in death. I will not
let you keep them, I will
replace them with brutal marbles.

I have plans for you,
plans to empty you,
to reshape your shell into
that thing I once read about,
that thing a little like you
at your most robust,
in the shimmy before
a pounce, a yellow snarl
dripping from its gums,
a tremor on its brow,
ink eclipsing its eyes.

Death retracted your terror,
your claws—made you tractable.
I'll make you wild, once more,

stuff you full
of wood wool and wire
so you'll hold the pose,
that familiar symmetry.

Monster Mother

Although the infants were distressed by these pointed rebuffs, they simply
waited until the spikes receded and then returned and clung to the mother.

—Professor Harry F. Harlow, 1965

He called her *monster mother*
and I imagine he was proud
to sneak silliness like that
into his study—a hiccup
in the quotidian. The truth is
he opened a thing's skin
and never intended on calling
what he had done
a wound,
and then everyone said
it was science, and then everyone
tried it for themselves
because the scientific method
said so, and so they perpetuated
an arrogance of dreams, of believing
that everything we touch
ought to turn into what we want,
and that somehow the touching
is all right.

He called her *monster mother*
because her belly growled
with sharpness—knives and nails
and points. He called her
monster mother because
he hid pointed tools in her

47

to punish the baby—*her* baby—
for not knowing most hugs
don't hurt like that.
He called her *monster mother*
because he hid his tools in her
to punish the baby
for hugging her, anyway,
over and over and over.
It never occurred to the baby
not to love, and it never
occurred to him to call it love
and stop.

The Tour Guide

after Brian DeLae's "What Once Was"

Look, to the right you'll notice
his architecture jutting the dune
like some half-swallowed dream,
another hubris reduced
by the gentle violence of millennia.

In this image, time and sand
thump heavy against an analogy
about an hourglass. Something
about how years blur meaning
into memory, memory into nostalgia,
nostalgia into a voyeuristic notion
of the-way-things-used-to-be
and, finally, into forty-five seconds
of a tour guide's spiel. Here is a truth
about hackneyed things: they sprawl
on our collective tongue, tunneling
into familiar vernacular
for a reason. For an intellectual,
it's embarrassing to admit that, yes,
everyone else was right
and they have been for a long time.

In the deep belly of this desert,
skyscrapers quiet into skeletal metropolis—
a graveyard of arrogantly-named things.
This vestige of that cityscape
scarcely pokes our ground, which was

their sky. And isn't that quaint?
There is humor in humbled ambition,
so let's laugh at Ozymandias, at Icarus,
at anyone else trying to scratch sky.

The Other Three Pigs

In a different story, the animals conspire
to become wolf by draping a cloak
over their hulk and growling at women
who pass on the street. Everyone is convinced
the pigs are human. A real man high, high up
in a skyscraper sees the three-pigged man, notices
the lovely pink peeking from the cloak, and hurries
to offer the piggybacked pigs a pair of bootstraps
to pull themselves up by; a corner office; a certificate
of self-worth signed by everyone in the land; a list
of everything they're allowed to take, which is simply
a list of everything in the land, albeit one
with women's names in bold and in one-point-larger font;
a Tinder profile seeking women in the area, which
is a conditional offering that, if refused,
renders all the other offerings void; a ticket
to a workshop on proper dick-pic protocol; a *spoiler*
on that workshop, which is that the answer is early, often,
and always; an offhand racist remark; a clap
on the back and a chortle to emphasize the remark
and its humor; a pair of New Balance sneakers;
a Tonka truck for their son; oodles of double standards
for their daughter; a dog because cats are pussies,
for pussies; another clap and chortle for obvious reasons;
a backstory with just enough disappointment
that they are certain they can't possibly be privileged
and that privilege is a dirty, dirty lie; and, lastly,
a large pile of feed because they are just pigs, after all.

The Hunter

The hulking crack of a rifle. The mountain lion static, then electric—a hive of impulse. Right. Bolt right. A muscular stumble into barbed wire. A quick knot. A raspy bellow. Red. Red. Again. A raspy bellow. The hulking crack of a rifle. Quiet now.

In a different story, the hunter names the cat and, in the time it takes to name, misses. It's easy to aim at an unnamed thing. Or is it simply convenient?

Eviction

Three years have passed
since I inherited this house,
his hockshop chock full of trinkets.

I make my way past a hodgepodge
of pocket watches, cufflinks, rings, lockets
huddled behind a window display.

Around the neck of a mannequin,
an assortment of cross necklaces
knot to a sterling Star of David.
It is not an optimism but a reminder
that all holiness is hand-me-down—
that I am the curator of unwanted things.

Nestled between a Matryoshka doll
and a stuffed sea turtle
with a missing marble eye,
I find his urn, turn it to see
what comes out.

Cleaning the House

She scratches him still, lovingly
tries to unearth a purr, but
he scratches back, scuttling

to me.

There is caterwaul
between us.

She buries her face in fur
to muffle syllables she swears
are language. Again, scratches.

These days, I do not tickle
the supper bell, or click
my tongue, or even rub
the belly dangerously: I pull
the cat's tail. Unequivocal.
She understands.

Later, I'll clean the house.
Later, I'll vacuum.

But now we speak cat. I scratch
between his ears:
Occasionally, he thrums.
Occasionally, he runs away.
He is unreliable or perceptive.
I'll decide later.

I Was Innocent After All

The first time we met, I told her
who she was to me, which is to say
I altered her, stuffed her
to a template, took her body
and squished the shoulder blades—
even broke them—massaged the legs
a little longer than she'd like,
kneaded each part just so
because she didn't fit without that
bit of elbow grease. Years later,
she told me she noticed, told me
she felt her edges urge uncomfortably
towards my words. She told me
I had been good incorrectly, again.
Of course, I agreed. Of course,
I asked if I could help, if I could
step into her nostalgia to unspool
the monster I was to her. Mine
wasn't an innocent gesture.
I wanted, as always, to be cared for,
to be worried about, to be told
I was innocent, after all.

The Fall

A maple tree in fall is temporary
heaven, bursting celebratory
against dull, gray sky. Each leaf
suffocates to earn that violent orange.
The damage is gentle and wildly
beautiful. I'd make the analogy
but I'm pretty sure you know
what this is about: there is aftermath
to every type of happiness—we all know it.
Soon, say, after a storm, the maple's leaves
will stick like chewed-up, spit-out confetti,
coating streets, sidewalks, everything
in slow rot, in papier-mâchéd autumn.
There is something primordial in this
falling off—in the beauty above
becoming mulch beneath our boots.
Something satisfying, too—like knowing
Eden crumbled under the weight
of an inquiry. Even in God's own story,
that's how it happened. I think this is why
fall is my favorite season; it reminds us
that everything, even miracles, unspools.
All it takes is time and gentle,
the gentlest suffocation.

The Cost of an Egg

Picture your best barn.
It's blunt red, lulling
in a field like some dream.
A procession of plump white clouds
scrolls above in impossibly blue sky.
All the colors in your landscape
are primary and inevitable.

Inside the barn, each animal
follows that script we all know:
Chickens rove, peck at bits
and seeds that skim the dirt.
They are jittering, idiot,
happy creatures here.
In the corner, a hen
warms a crown of eggs
under her soft weight,
a chestnut horse brays
and dangles his great head
out the edge of his stall.
The orange barn cat
snakes your ankles, trumpeting
her hunger over and over—
it almost seems she could leave,
but, no, hunger is easier here.
If you squint, you'll see the wild
in this barn. If you squint harder,
all you'll see is human.

Lewis

The first time I loved him,
his exaggerated ears flattened
as he peeked out the window pane.
A robin pecked at bits and birdseed,
while, inside, he traced her jig, slunk
so low his whiskers combed the floor,
unaware his hind betrayed him, swaying
and upright. He shimmied, shimmied,
spasmed into a pounce—clawed &
bushy-tailed—at the red-bellied bird.
He crashed against glass, then scuttled
the stairs to hide in the dark.

My father told me the saddest stories
are not about broken things—no,
the saddest stories are the happy ones
told in past tense because we know
everything is broken and we have
to see it untouched first, we have
to do the breaking ourselves.
I think that's true.

The moment I loved him
he was already past tense, and I
already expected broken things—
the slur of his aging body,
the way he'd misremember
a movement, the way his skin
would clench firm to skeleton,

the way each sleep would look
like a destination, the way life
quietly turns life-like, and how
that is maybe the saddest part,
or, no, the way he'd become
precious, which is the gentle way
to say ruined, or, no, the way
I'm saying goodbye
and he's still right here.

The Trouble Is

The trouble is
every cat is Lewis
if given the name
and time enough
to break
       and break
the boy's heart.
The trouble is
most cats are just cats
and break
       and break
enough times
to be a number,
not a name.
The trouble is
we know this.
The other trouble is
we prefer the number.

Only You

after Stephen Dunn's "Instead of You"

Where I am going there is no image
to pin to a page
like a black, gold butterfly—
there is only you,
and you, I know, will struggle.

I don't have a bait & switch,
or patience for your watermark
to enter the poem, but
I do have a cat and I do have a you.

Butterflies are hard enough:
they'll dart and flit to avoid the net
like (what was it?) a bat
trapped in sunlight, but,
eventually, everything
leads to a wound. If that sounds
like wisdom, please know
it is not; I am only trying
to get to you
in my own way, but

you are tougher to swat—
and I can't pin it on the cat—
because you are so beautiful,
and there are so few words
for so beautiful (admittedly,
a lot of clichés). Is this
where the drops of blood lead:
To your shadow, carcassed

on this page, pinned like a blur
of a body—somebody
once worth keeping?

Yes, I'm afraid
it is too late
for this
to be our love poem.

The Heart Is Vestigial

This is the hardest part,
but watch: all surgery
is inspired by torture.
I snap a toothbrush.
The bristle is now
the handle, and
the half-shaft left
is now sharp enough
to scalpel. A broken
toothbrush is not a tool
for easy surgery.

In the strictest sense,
science can makeshift
a heart. So, in those
strictest senses,
the heart is vestigial.

But something belongs, right?
Something that's necessary
to make what's human
tock. How much surgery
before the toothbrush
nicks it?

Lie down. Let me cut
along your dotted lines.

Cow

Afterbirth hangs from her—
it might dangle there for days
like snakeskin until it drops,
but this time the bull sniffs,
tugs at it, clamps his teeth to the pink,
and yanks. He grinds it down,
and swallows.

The way he rips, the way she shudders:
it's easy to hate him.

                         Be careful, though.

The next scent of birthing blood
might bring coyotes to yank, to rip,
again, but not like him—he stopped.

They leave nothing
to interpret.

Blue Jeans

I was once young enough
to dry-hump with a straight face,
unaware how years
would squeeze hindsight
between our blue-jeaned chafe,
how they would tell us it was silly
to keep our flesh so far apart,
but there is romance in struggle,
in the ancient lust of the untouched
intent on the unseen. I have loved
through blue jeans—nothing
has been pure since.

What We Are Inside

Picture your best skeleton.
Look, the sharp edge of bone
sloppily makes an image—surely
that is invitation enough
to detect a humanity
haunting the shape of skull, haunting
the billow of ribcage, the needle
of femur and fibula. At night,
you might even swear it were a real boy
if you squint and scare easily.

What I am trying to say is, yes,
flesh is a generous interpretation
of the bone beneath. It's no wonder
we've found a way to find beauty
in the soft stuff the same way we polish
and polish memory into nostalgia—
such gorgeous erasure. But the scaffolding,
that deeper thing with yawning eyeholes
and a politician's grin, that dull
white filling inches beneath skin
is menace, unequivocal. And isn't that
something like commentary? If skeleton
is not analogy for the self, then dammit
if I won't make it one. Watch me.

No, what I meant to say was better
than this. Something about how deliberate
the ugliness is. Something about that
not mattering when we ignore it, or feed it, or

pretend that it behaves. What I meant to say wasn't
that it's hard to see the human in the skeleton.
What I meant to say was the opposite of that.
What I meant to say was beware.

The Old Snow Leopard

In dreams, the elk are willing.
They find dull rocks to begin
the suffocation themselves.

The snow leopard, a bundle
of rubber bands, whispers
toward the huddle of elk,

who are already lightheaded,
aloof, and waiting to run
slowly enough to be caught.

The old snow leopard uncoils,
leaps an underwater leap—
deliberate, exaggerated,

easy on the joints. The elk
sleepwalk away—a courtesy
to make it feel real.

The snow leopard wants a hunt,
understand. In dreams,
he has teeth still.

In dreams, he is not glazed
with old age. He is menace.
He has meaning.

Enough Like Love

At twilight, he trumpets
his hunger, snakes at my ankles,
tries to shepherd me
towards the food dish. His habit
feels enough like love
to call it love.

Lost Cat

Only affection should tether.
Things that tether anyway: not affection.
It is tautology, which means it bears repeating,
bears repeating. There is something quite different—
subterranean, even—about a missing cat.
Gravestones come to mind. Bandages require wounds
or is only the opposite true?

Sleepy gods still dream existence. Everything is breaking still.

Everything is as true as it is sonically appealing.
Even the cat is not literal. It is always about night.
A cat is a half-crescent stretch. It is a critter with fleas.
It is harder to deal with than not to.

I am speaking about myself, too.

I want to haunt the image of a cat, swim deep within its vapor.
I'm lonely for my cat. There is something trapped in the twilight.
I think it is. Other pronouns are rabid with condolences
for the things I've lost. Empathy is an impossible task.
They are silly for taking it up, stupid for thinking it possible,
and so, so guilty for declaring it obvious. I am lonely for my cat.

How to Be Afraid

I am not afraid
of a bottomless pit—
I'd make a life
on the way down.
No, the pit I fear
is the one I know
I fall exactly as long
as I am afraid to fall,
where the thing to fear
is not being afraid.

Disposal

You have to touch the body
at least one last time. And
you have to start calling it
the body, not *his* body.

You have to scoop the body up.
It will do everything it can
to get back
to the ground—
this is gravity, not intent.

The Story I Tell

 My father found the cat
broken, tonguing the burst of red
on his forepaw
in slow, deliberate licks.
His neck rocked in clockwork:
back & forth, back & forth.
This is medicine a cat knows,
but it won't work this time.
This time the burst is cancer.
This time the cat is dying.

My father never told me
how heavy the dying cat was,
he never told me what it took
to lift a thing like that,
and I never asked
how to touch what's left,
how to carry what's left
to the car, or whether
tenderness still worked
on a body in goodbye,
and I never asked
if the cat cried
the whole ride there
like he always had before
or if, this time, he kept at his work:
back, forth, back, forth.

And that's the story I tell.
The truth is

I found the cat first,
saw the way his body
touched the ground
like an awful spill,
and I called
what I saw there sleep,
so I left
because I couldn't
bring myself
to rise him.

How to Make a Heart

This is how to make a heart:

Stick four thick-cut straws
into a fistful of raw pork.
Pretend to squeeze
involuntarily. Count up
to your least favorite number.

Stop squeezing.

A Hum of Movement

In the nighttime, I construct my last cat's ghost. I start with the skeleton, bending slender light into a spine, a skull, ribcage, then continue to organs and fur, the button drops of black on his coat. I tickle static into the body—a hum of movement. I hoist the memory and feel warmth.

There are worse things than an old cat becoming a dead one. I do not try to count those things. Here in my hands his ghost is content and impossibly weighted. I know he cannot stay. I breathe his body. He unspools into the moonlight.

The Moment Before

In every type of happiness she knows,
she knows it's dangerous to smile
because afterwards is violent
like, say, the rapture of flight
corrupted by buckshot, like
a burst of red, lovely
until the broken skin, or that
fiddle-leaf fig, handsome
as an accent in the corner
of the room, but, closer,
there is rot at the stems,
a gentle suffocation.

She's thinking of instinct, the one
convincing a moth to the light—
is it ever more certain
than in the moment before
its body unspools? No, she thinks.

Her young lover is an assemblage
of toothpicks and feathers
and matchlight—a temporary
heaven. He's thinking beautifully
of the hollow bones of angels.
He's drunk on the fragility
of their flight. How wondrous
to be weak, he thinks.

His own weakness is stunning—
he is crescendo, he is luminescence.

He is the endless pursuit of up, is Icarus
clawing towards sun, is that moth,
stiff in the moment before.

I Put Him on the Floor

There is a dead cat.
Yes, I put him
on the floor
of my mind. It is
an appropriate leap
to imagine him there—
most cats extinguish
on the floor. Okay,
I slide bones into him.
They are too big
to slide in like splinters,
but this is a dream,
is a dream, is a dream
recurring.

Book Unhinged

A man has died
his house is tidy
too tidy to be
happenchance
he prepared
ordered things
catalogued
their final
resting places
but there is one
book unhinged—
his last hello.

My Father Says

My father says not to name him,
       says we cannot keep the cat,
       says he is half blind, toothless,
       too soon from a mother to keep,
       says we cannot give him
       what he needs, says the clinic
       costs more than the cat is worth,
       says not to name him
       because a man is cuffed
       to the things he names,
       says not to name him
       because naming a cat
       does not make him ours,
       it makes him us—
but I call him Lewis.

Notes

"Look How Obedient They Are": The phrase "heaven of animals" references James Dickey's poem of the same name.

"The Rapture": The allusion to Robert Hass is a reference to "Meditation at Lagunitas."

"Broken Alchemy": The mention of Robert Frost references his poem "Nothing Gold Can Stay."

"Monster Mother" references a series of scientific studies conducted by Harry F. Harlow wherein he researched the psychological effects of maternal-separation, dependency needs, and social isolation on infant rhesus monkeys.

Acknowledgements

Poems or iterations of poems in this book were originally published in these books and journals: *Tin House* ("Like a Gift), *The Missouri Review* ("The Rapture), *Rattle* ("My First Body Is Beautiful Until"), *Ninth Letter* ("Forgive Me, I Am a Violent Shape"), *Cimarron Review* ("My Neighbor's Cat), *Barrelhouse* ("The Magic"), *Moon City Review* ("Thank You"), *Spillway* ("A Hum of Movement"), *Fifth Wednesday Journal* ("Misunderstanding"), *Cactus Heart* ("The Hunter"), *Punchnel's* ("The Things Fathers Get to Remember" & "A Little Like Desire"), *Zetetic: A Record of Unusual Inquiry* ("The Chipmunk"), *Third Wednesday* ("Dead Tiger"), *Four Chambers Press* ("Cow"), *In Sight: An Ekphrastic Collaboration* ("Look How Obedient They Are"), *Big Muddy: A Journal of the Mississippi River Valley* ("The Heart Is Vestigial"), *The Cape Rock: Poetry* ("Bring Flowers to What You Love"), *Cider Press Review* ("The Other Three Pigs" & "Monster Mother").

While this book bears my name, it would not have been possible without those who have hoisted me along the way. That begins with all of the editors at *Cider Press Review* for choosing my manuscript as the winner of the 2020 *Cider Press Review* Editors' Prize Book Award. I also want to thank Joe Paris, the teacher who introduced me to poetry in the first place; Richard Conner, my father who supported me at every step and in every way; my incredible professors, Sally Ball, Henri Cole, Norman Dubie, Beckian Fritz Goldberg, Andrew Hudgins, Terry Hummer, Tara Ison, and Alberto Rios; my gracious readers and friends, Lauren Albin, Jackie Balderrama, Brian Bender, Steve Boggins, Mindy Burkhardt, Alexandra Comeaux, Tori Conner, Anna Dye, Courtney Fowler, Gary "Josh" Garrison, Ben Glass, Melissa Goodrich, Bryan Patton, and Cameron Wells who kindly responded to the many, many poems I sent them over the years; my lovely and supportive partner, Mimi Tyree; the rest of my family, Owen Conner, Halle Rex, Jane Rex, Amanda Tyree, Gary Tyree, Hala Tyree, Keith Tyree, Bill Wells, and Drew Wells; and, of course, the cats I have and the ones I have lost along the way: Lewis, Puffer, Bugsbee, Trooper, Yeti, Kiki, Lili, and my beloved Pretzel.

Thank you all.

About the Author

Reese Conner received his M.F.A. from Arizona State University, where he has continued to teach composition and poetry. His creative work appears in *Tin House, The Missouri Review, Ninth Letter, Barrelhouse, New Ohio Review,* and elsewhere.

Reese received the Turner Prize from the Academy of American Poets, the Mabelle A. Lyon Poetry Award, and the now-defunct Chili Pepper from Rate My Professor. He was a finalist for the 2019 New American Poetry Prize, the 2019 *Cider Press Review* Book Award, and his poetry has been nominated for a Pushcart Prize.

Reese lives in Tucson, Arizona with his partner and their three well-proportioned cats.